GOD'S WISDOM AND VIRGIL'S POETRY IN RHYME

Virgil Sturgeon

ISBN 979-8-88644-923-5 (Paperback)
ISBN 979-8-88644-924-2 (Digital)

Covenant Books
11661 Hwy 707
Murrells Inlet, SC 29576
www.covenantbooks.com

Strength
and honor are
her clothing;... She
looketh well to the ways
of her household,...Her
children arise up and
call her blessed;...
Prov. 31:25-28

CONTENTS

Heritage Greens

INTRODUCTION

In February 2022, I received a message from JESUS in a dream that occurred in my sleep one night after my wife, Janet, had passed away. In that dream or vision, I spoke directly to JESUS.

HE called out my name, "Virgil, I want you to go to HERITAGE GREENS in GREENSBORO, NORTH CAROLINA."

I remember replying, "Yes, LORD, I will go where You send me. But why there, LORD?"

HE replied, "There is someone I want you to meet!"

I answered by saying, "How will I know this person?"

There was a quiet pause, and then JESUS replied, "I WILL SEND HER TO YOU."

That was the end of our conversation and the dream!

My incredible interpretation of God's message and prophetic dream

A few weeks later, my son Lonny enrolled me as a resident of Heritage Greens in Greensboro, North Carolina. I was struggling with severe back problems at the time of my arrival, and in fact, the three bad disks in my lower back had me confined to a wheelchair with future hopes of improvement and walking again questionable at best. Little did I realize how incredibly near that future hope was at my time of arrival at Heritage Greens.

Upon establishing this as my new residence, I took up a meeting with an established group every evening after dinner at the same location in the atrium hall and became good friends with the group, enjoying the fellowship, stories, and laughter that abounded. The group even inspired my poem writing, and I firmly believe that was the point at which GOD resurrected that blessing HE had bestowed on my life as a part of HIS overall plan formulated back in 1947.

I remember distinctly sitting in my wheelchair, one evening, listening to a music program being presented and wishing I could get out of my wheelchair and dance to the music as I used to when from behind me came this voice, saying, "VIRGIL, let's dance."

I looked over my shoulder and immediately recognized the person as a member of the regular meeting group. She was a young lady whom everyone called MJ.

I remember saying to MJ, "I can't move and control my feet and legs!"

She said, "Have you tried?"

I replied, "Well, no, I haven't."

She said, "GET UP OUT OF YOUR WHEELCHAIR, and let's dance!"

Do you know that I got out of the wheelchair and danced two dances with MJ!

That evening, after retiring to my room, I sat down at my computer and compiled a poem titled "MY MIRACLE COME TRUE" (included in the book). GOD was truly at work and preparing me for completing His plan for my future book of poems and the other phase of the planned project. He also injected MJ (Mary Jo) into the picture, and she became the one who reviewed all of my newly written poems, gave her opinion, and even suggested I seek out a book publisher! It was during this period of indecision that I began to consider publishing a book of poetry!

Mary Jo was a big supporter and consistently loyal and dedicated, and I relied heavily on her opinions and judgment. Her career background as an educator and her Christian faith gave me the confidence I needed to cautiously proceed! Another young lady of honorable mention and great assistance was a young student. I will call her Kay. She was employed by Heritage Greens and was working while attending college. She donated her time to type up my poems, making them presentable to be sent to my publishing company for inclusion in the projected poem book. I believe God will bless all who helped with the book in ways yet to come, and in fact, that is my fervent and ongoing prayer!

The first process was to come up with a name for the book that would enhance publication sales and distribution. There was no doubt in my mind that God had to be acknowledged; after all, it was His original game plan! So what better title than *God's Wisdom and Virgil's Poetry in Rhyme*?

It turns out to be a wise decision because the publisher chosen turns out to be a Christian publisher and distributor to outlets worldwide—a publisher named Covenant Books.

This pretty well convinced me of this fact: IF you glorify our GOD, HE will bless you in ways that are beyond human comprehension. HIS ultimate goal is worldwide acceptance and for mankind, whom HE created, to be an example throughout HIS UNIVERSE.

Even though some of the poems written and included are works as far back as 1947, this book will tie in with a later publication of a future AUTOBIOGRAPHY by Virgil to be titled *The Untold Story Can Now Be Told*. Virgil also anticipates a second volume of his poetry now that it's in the production stages! So hang on tight, and ENJOY Virgil's poetry and GOD's coming message to the WORLD!

OLD GLORY

Our flag! Old Glory

From each state that's represented here

They've died to keep "old glory"

And its thirteen stripes of red appear to remind
    us of its story for on a field of royal blue

Her fifty stars keep shining true

A monument, red, white, and blue is
    the flag we call Old Glory

Down through the years, free men will
    stand in tribute to Old Glory

While 'round the world, her helping hand adds
    pages to life's story, for on a field of
royal blue her fifty stars are forever true—a
    monument, red, white, and blue is the flag
we call Old Glory

Our children, young, have yet to learn
    the meaning of Old Glory

Yet if they're called, they'll take their turn to stand
    beside Old Glory, and though I pray,
I'll never see the day they face an enemy I know,
    should God grant victory, he'll grant it
to Old Glory

JESUS IS OUR LIGHTHOUSE

JESUS is the lighthouse that shines so all may see
a world that's filled with gloom and doubt
HIS love is there for free.
HE calms the fearful heart and soul
that grieves a loss divine, of a love
that only soulmates know
and will share through eternal time
That LIGHTHOUSE, firm on rocky shores,
above life's stormy seas, to light the path we all must
trek, along life's given way.
Oh! What a blessing for mankind,
That LIGHTHOUSE shows the way.
HE stands upon life's rocky shores
and lights the path each day.

OUR BATTLE
FROM WITHIN

He speaks to us in many ways,
His wisdom to reveal,
Express your feelings from within,
For love ye shan't conceal,
No matter what the conscience says,
Our hearts will dare reveal,
It's just our nature—the way we're made—
for love we shan't conceal,
So try with all the strength you can,
To go another way,
You'll find it is the way of man,
And love will rule the day,
So don't suppress those feelings,
That come from deep within,
God sets our course,
We have no choice,
It is His law for man.
No matter if we think in error,
That conscience is our friend,
It goes against God's given plan,
For love will always win,
So express those feelings,

Deep within,
And love do not conceal,
Be true to self and trust,
In God—just let the heart reveal,
Our course is set—He shows the way,
And knows when love is real,
Remember it's His law for man,
True love you never conceal.

OUR DESTINATION

Take the bountiful life we've been granted,
And multiply that by a score,
Then witness a life that's enchanted,
With beauty to last evermore,
Just envision a picture before you,
Of glory with peace so divine,
The sands of time that are sprinkled with gold dust,
That glimmers with hope throughout time,
That's the promise our God has projected,
His word for eternity is true,
To guide all His children who love Him,
Sinners like me and like you,
So give our God honor and glory,
And be true and faithful, my friend,
His promises never forsaken,
Eternity awaits,
There's no end.

August 21, 2022

MEMORY

When I was just a lad of four,
And at my grandpa's place,
My mind retains a memory,
Of family, love, and grace,
I fell into a pool of mud,
That caused my mother stress,
You see, there was no change of clothes,
Except for my auntie's dress,
So the dress I wore throughout the day,
With dignity, I'm told,
My mind retains that memory,
Now that I'm growing old,
A memory that lives so strong,
From a time long, long ago,
It reinvigorates,
Those precious hours,
Of family, love, and grace,
To be recalled on heaven's shore,
At a special time and place.

August 28, 2022

ETERNITY, TRAVEL, AND TIME

Since God called her home to our heaven,
My soulmate will never more roam,
Except in our travels together,
Seeking eternities home,
A beautiful preview of glory,
We'll savor its love so divine,
As we travel the *eons* before us,
And marvel at creation's design,
The universe ever expanding,
New galaxies formed over time,
For we give our God honor and glory,
And marvel at creation's design.

August 28, 2022

THE DESTINY OF TYRANTS

Men of wanton,
Men of greed,
Why must your foolish souls and cold,
stone hearts of sin exceed,
The want of peace,
The whole world has.
A world where lives are filled with love,
And dreams pursued,
From *Him* above,
Go, sons of Satan,
Spread your hate,
For *God* above still holds your fate,
And as your day of judgment nears,
Sweet peace will drown out all our fears,
A cheery world will once more strive,
For things unheard of,
Things untried,
And men will live, and love, and die,
In peace forevermore.

August 28, 2022

THE ATRIUM

In the hall of loving friendship,
Where mercy does abound,
We gather daily from life's tasks,
And share a common ground,
Today's survival is our goal,
In fact it's number one,
Without it we would be no more,
We might totally succumb,
To set aside the challenges,
God places all around,
In the hall of loving friendship,
Where mercy does abound.

In the hall of loving friendship where Jesus does abide,
Where thoughts and memories of our past,
We share with foolish pride,
Each act of love recorded,
On heaven's scroll of life,
Gives all the hope and grace we need,
To wipe away our strife,
To gather every evening,
And share our thoughts and love,
In the hall of loving friendship,

That is sent from those above,
We set aside the challenges,
God places all around,
In the hall of loving friendship,
Where mercy does abound,
So come and share your moments,
Of love, and peace, and grace,
In the hall of loving friendship,
Make it your meeting place.

August 28, 2022

A WORD OF GOD'S WISDOM AND TRUTH

*The Difference from a Dream and
God's Prophesies from Old*

A dream is a vision compiled by the mind
And is set by the mind so as to view
And in likeness, we find a "real-life" event
Formed of memories that seem real and true
Now GOD's prophesies we find are
    much different, of course
For they're based on HIS wisdom divine
Remembering HIS plan of creation, with no true remorse
That HE knows the present, the future,
    and the past over time
Time HE controls as the future unfolds to
    the plan HE made for mankind
HE prophesies actions that are needed to fulfill
    some future event from HIS mind
And they are set to come true, without any adieu,
    within the time of HIS choosing to do

So you can be sure that the prophecy made
    will be fulfilling a part of the plan
And is definitely set to come true
Remember, dreams fade away, being
    formed in man's mind
And are set by the mind so to view
GOD's prophesies filled, ensure HIS plan is on track
Guaranteed to ALWAYS come true

ETERNAL LOVE DIVINE

Sixty-nine years and counting
Back to 1952
In a little chapel on Holliday Street
Reserved for me and you

We shared our dreams, exchanged our vows,
And started life anew
From that little chapel on Holliday Street
In June of '52

From the playgrounds of old High Street
To the wide Pacific blue
We've traveled o'er the USA
In search of dreams come true

And generations later, and a great-great-grandson, too
Our love has stood the test of time since 1952

The moral of this story is that dreams can still come true
Just put your trust and faith in God, for He will see you
through
For I believe with all my heart, eternity will prove
Our union was no accident back in 1952

June 2021

THIS MOMENT IS MINE
TO SHARE AND ATTEST

I retire to the porch with my eyes looking west
The day is over and the old rocking chair is put to its test
Caressing each tired and aching muscle
And this moment is mine to share and attest
The sun dips below the horizon
The keeper and controller of time at its best
A deep blue haze outlines the majestic Alleghenies
And this moment is mine to share and attest
A golden aurora gently kisses the evening sky goodnight
Another glorious day slips beyond the sunset to rest
And retires to eternity soothed and caressed
And this moment is mine to share and attest
My mind takes a snapshot and I savor the sweetness thereof
Giving honor and glory, for I know that I'm blessed
And this moment is mine to share and attest

BEAUTY OF THE SEASONS

While strolling through the countryside, upon the hills I see
In red, green, brown, and amber hues miss autumn's lingerie
The wonders never cease to be; it's magic to behold
The way that God has blended all the red, green, brown,
    and gold

Yet autumn's just another sign, dame winter's coming nigh
To spread her silvery ermine cloak around us from on high
And in her long and stormy reign, a great new year is born
With a loving personality, buds and blossoms shall adorn

Then as the spring is changing into summer's golden way
We should realize the beauty that surrounds us every day
There're those I know who never see these treasures that
    abound
And yet the only secret is: lift the eyes and look around

Copyright November 8, 1989

ETERNITY

With the universe ever expanding
To far reaches yet to be known
With new stars being planted
New galaxies being sown
One universe if there is an end
And if one day we'll see
An end to God's creation
And His eternity
Think not, for He has
Plans for man
A future yet unknown
Exploring His glorious,
Universe, providing creations home
We ponder not the reason
Nor speculate just why
We use the knowledge He projects
Keep your eye upon the sky!

ETERNITY AWAITS US ALL

These words to be exalted as an honor to my wife
Who gave her all to family love;
Who lived the perfect life,
Her mission now on heaven's shore,
There was no truer friend,
I patiently await the call,
To reunite again;
Be still, my heart, and comfort me,
As I receive my loss,
The soulmate God assigned for me,
Now lies beneath the cross,
Her mission here on earth complete,
According to God's plan
To spread His words of joy and peace,
To love your fellow man,
For in the realm of knowledge known,
As God's omnipotent word,
Lies promises as yet fulfilled,
And music yet unheard,
So take this message straight from Him;
This life is not the end,
Eternity awaits our souls,
The journey just begins.

A MOUNTAIN STREAM

A mountain stream to me, o world
Is like the future yet unfurled

Its dark deep pools of sad dismay
Its sparkling rapids dance and play

Its green-rimmed banks shine through a mist
Of rainbow colors sunshine kissed

Its stones unturned, its falls from high
Beneath an ever-changing sky

Leaves me with this one thought supreme
The future's like a mountain stream

Copyright November 23, 1989

DREAMS

When I get rich and big enough
There're things I'm going to do
I'm going to fly about the world
And sail each ocean blue

I'm going to fill an album
With photos of new friends
And ask that they might share with me
A love that never ends

I'll build a giant castle
On a bluff above the Rhine
That overlooks a valley
Where the sun will always shine

I'm going to share with those in need
A portion of my wealth
In hopes that it will bring to all
A measure of good health

This world's in need of others
Who would share such dreams as me
When I get rich and big enough
Well, just you wait and see

22

THE FATE OF MAN

Memories of the past to treasure
Never let them go
Like photos from an old, old album
Enrich our heritage so.
This life on earth is but a moment
Cast on endless time
And meant for us to fully savor
Each moment so divine.
To live this life in all its fullness
To capture what you can.
Eternity, unknown, awaits us
God knows the fate of man.
Each action we perform enhances
The eternal plan.
That He in all His grace and glory
Crafted by His hand.
So savor every given moment
Contribute what you can
Eternity, for sure, awaits
It is the fate of man.
And here's the deal, He won't reveal
What we cannot understand.
The Written Word will clearly suffice
He'll show us when He can.

THE SMILE

A smile is just another blessing
In a world of woe and strife
Yet marvel at the power it holds
To even change one's life
That pleasant gesture, labor free
So few can ever resist
Returns rewards for to unfold
Your ego so to lift
So share this blessing God provides
Enjoy life while you can
It's just another way to say
I love my fellow man!

GOD'S BLESSING UNFOLDS

The rain's tomorrow's blessing
For the flowers that are yet to come
Whose seed lies dormant beneath the soil
Awaiting Springtime's Sun
The tender seedling reaches upward, hungry for the air
And plants its roots and stakes its claim
Creations fame to share
'Tis like a chain reaction, making everyone aware
As tender seedlings springing forth, it seems from everywhere
And soon to come forth, vibrant colors of flowers of
    every kind
That saturates the landscape and stimulates the mind
It's hard to fathom such a blessing coming from just one
Blessed and cooling rain shower that GOD just gave for FUN

January 9, 2023

COURAGE ON DISPLAY

The body sometimes racked with pain,
Becomes the driving force
To overcome adversity by showing no remorse;
For obstacles encountered
In the tasks we face each day;
Become the challenge of the hour to find a simpler way,
The "Breath of Life" gives us the hope
To work toward a way,
To do the tasks we're meant to do,
But just another way;
So when you see these struggles
Of sheer courage on display
Stand up and cheer them onward,
With a big hip, hip hooray!

KITCHY-KATOO

I walked downtown the other day
I had a little shopping to do
I passed this store with a great big sign
It said here's something for you

Well, they had these beans in a big glass jar
The prize was a Kitchy-Katoo
I said "gee whiz, I'm going to win that prize
'cause counting is something I can do"

Well, I bought me some beans and I started to count
I counted till I nearly turned blue
The man walked up and said "what you got?"
I said "fourteen thousand and two, man,
        fourteen thousand and two"

Now he gave a little grin and he turned around
And handed me the Kitchy-Katoo
I said "gee thanks, I sure feel proud
'cause winning for me's something new"

So I took them on home now, I'm scratching my head
'cause I don't know quite what to do
I'm using those doggone beans all right
But what the heck does a Kitchy-Katoo do?
What the heck is a Kitchy-Katoo?

Well, it's small 'n' round, weighs less than a pound
And is kind of a powdery blue
If anyone knows, please give me a call
And tell me just what does it do

Now if you ever run into a situation
Involving a Kitchy-Katoo
Well, take my advice and ask kind of nice
What the heck does a Kitchy-Katoo do?
What the heck is a Kitchy-Katoo?

THE CHRISTIAN CRITTERS

We are the Christian Critters and we want it to be told.
We've got the love of Jesus in our hearts and in our souls.
We love to get together in any kind of weather.
To build our faith and with God's grace
His kingdom we'll unfold.

Yes, we're the Christian Critters and we want to make it
    clear.
We'll spread the love of Jesus to our friends throughout the
    year.
The time we share with Jesus will fill our hearts with cheer.
We'll build our faith and with God's grace.
We'll bring His kingdom near.

Amen. Amen. Amen. Amen.
Amen. Amen. Amen.

THE ANSWERED PRAYER JESUS SENT TO HIS FATHER AND RESULTS OF HIS POWER OVER PRAYER

His chosen servant accepting the call
Will guarantee the success of the project, overall
So this prayer that HE invokes, giving thanks to the KING
    brings great joy for the heart, mind, and soul to recall
And these words of great wisdom won't fade
For it's truly a day the Lord's made
A day the LORD's made to record and to hold
As HIS prophesied story unfolds
Yes, we shout and rejoice, for our chance just to
    serve and be a part of this "story now told"

MOTHER'S DAY

Thousands of words have been written,
About mothers, so what can I do?
But write words of honor in fairness,
For you see, I really love two
One love is my birth mother, given by God,
The one that married my Pa.
The other—a blessing from heaven
That's known as my mother-in-law.
Now many bad jokes have been spoken
About mothers-in-law as you know.
But I'm here to give witness in writing,
That the picture they paint's just not so!
For a mother-in-law is a mother
And a mother is everyone's pride.
I'm proud of my mother and mother-in-law
That's a fact that I never will hide
All holidays hold special meaning
But none is so tender and dear
As that day that honors all mothers
A day we should always revere.

MY MIRACLE COMES TRUE

There are those that call her MJ
I'll call her Mary Jo.
To honor that God-given name
With personality aglow
She's been a friend that comforts me
When I was feeling low
So you can call her MJ
To me she's Mary Jo.
She raised me from my wheelchair
To dance a dance or two
It was more than just persuasion
It was a miracle come true
She guided me so gently
Encouraged me and so
You can call her MJ
I'll honor Mary Jo.

LIFE'S PLAN

When the breath of life's
First given
And the mind's completely clear
And this journey God lies
Out for us
Is the challenge
Oh so dear
Each day becomes a treasure
Of knowledge to behold
And store within an eager mind
On its way to growing old
We begin our earthly travel
On a path God only knows
And follow His instructions
With trust in where it goes
Each pathway that He chooses
Provides a different goal
In determining our future
On our way to growing old
So relax, enjoy what God
Has planned great adventures
To behold
It's the first stop to eternity
On our way to
Growing old.

OH, DEATH, WHERE IS YOUR STING

My treasured
Soulmate on this earth
You gave your all to me
I now await with
Patient heart that day
Again I'll be
Reunited with my love for all
Eternity
We'll travel over the
Universe in love
Forever true
Remembering those
Vows we made in 1952
For now we serve our
God in ways He chooses
Us to do, but death
Is but a short reprieve
His promises are true
My patient soul awaits
The time we reunite
In love while listening
To the heavenly hosts
And music from above

THE ULTIMATE MIND IS AT WORK ALL THE TIME

In Preparing the Judgment That's Promised and Due

GOD's ultimate MIND is at work ever more to
    garner memories of works from the past
HE uses the minds of HIS soul banks
    RESERVE, and it's the TRUTH
Like a mind of HIS own, to recall moments of TIME
Indelibly enshrined and engraved in
    those memories of past
Ever more to be stored and dependably true
Only HE can recall when it's due; for HIS judgment to fall
When fulfilling HIS LAW and HIS
    WORD so to last ever TRUE
For HEBREWS 9:27 is the law that says all
    and even HE must abide by its call
"And as it is appointed unto men, once to
    die, but after this, the judgment"
Will fall
GOD's creative mind is at work evermore in
    preparing for HIS promise to come

And His soul bank created for its use with mankind
Is a source for His JUDGMENT and call
For the soul remembers all, nothing escapes its recall
It's eternal, GOD made it to last
So in the end, what's embedded in the
       memory of the soul is GOD's
TRUTH
With the soul, there's no escape from the past
Though the soul, never seen
Is GOD's ultimate means of determining
       His judgment and call
ETERNITY awaits; it's never too late
For His mercy and LOVE covers all
Yes, it's never too late
Eternity awaits though some stumble,
       HE doesn't want them to fall

THE FINAL DOOR WE KNOW NOT WHY

We know not why
But once to die
Is the law set forth
For man
In Hebrews 9:27, we see
His word projects the plan
And then comes forth the judgment
We all must face for sure
And get our God's permission
To enter heaven's door
All sins to be forgiven
And love forevermore
So buckle up, the life
You live
Will be your judgment score
God gives no second chance
For this
It is the final door

THE HARVEST

In the quiet of our slumber
Or the busy of the day
Sometimes without a warning
A loved one's called away
And those who go before us
Rejoicing one and all
Lift up their souls to greater needs
When our work's all done, He'll call

Thus comes the ancient question
That's always asked ... Lord, why?
Remaining still unanswered
To those like you and I
We speculate and ponder
A mystery to us all
Whose answer lies beyond our reach
For when the work's all done, He'll call

And so we cherish memories
Of loved ones called away
Knowing that it's through our faith
We'll meet again someday
And like those gone before us
He beckons one and all
To joyously fulfill His needs
And when our work's all done, He'll call

REALITY BECKONS

If I could slow the pace of time,
Explore my every dream,
Expand the time to dwell in love,
Live life to the extreme,
It's just a fantasy I know,
A fleeting wish, a dream,
For God controls the universe,
Designed to meet man's needs,
His grace is never ending,
My wish reflects my greed,
A weakness born within myself,
Embedded in my seed,
We're never satisfied with what we have,
When grace is all we need,
I cannot slow the pace of time,
It's strictly God's control,
Perfection is His stated plan,
Embedded in *His* goal,
So I can fantasize and dream,
And never change the end,
God's Word is all we really need,
And His son *He* plans to send.

August 21, 2022

WINGS OF GOLD

Oh leave behind a memory
That will forever last
These moments flee on wings of gold
To an ever-hungry past
The present's just a moment grasped
But something we can't hold
For it glides beyond the sunset
On those fleeting wings of gold
In a world that's filled with sorrows
Joys and happiness sublime
Life is but a grain of sand
On the endless voids of time
So leave behind a memory
For the future to unfold
As you glide beyond the sunset
On those fleeting wings of gold

IF I COULD LIVE
LIFE OVER

When I was young and just a child
I knew not what to do
I did the very best I could
When starting out anew

If I could live life over
Some things would stay the same
And knowing of the end result
From others would refrain

I'd do the things I ought to do
Of that you can be sure
The live and learn philosophy's
Not easy to endure

I'd mind my manners when I'm told
And make a special rule
To do my homework every eve
And study hard in school

I'd volunteer to do
A little more than I was asked
And take my time to do things right
As opposed to being fast

I'd do my chores and store my toys
I'd help in any way
And feel that in so doing
It would make a better day

I'd tell the truth whenever asked
My conscience I would steer
For knowing right but doing wrong
Is something we should fear

I'd put away my temper
And observe the golden rule
For doing unto others
Is as precious as a jewel

There're many things as you can see
I'd do a different way
If I was young and knew the things
I know about today

Copyright November 22,1989

LIFE FOREVER BE
GOAL NUMBER ONE

We gather together in groups 'round the world
To answer His beck and HIS call
In rooms just like this, both large and some small
To honor THE CREATOR of all
THE WORD yet unheard, delivered by ANGELS
    and meant for mankind to recall
In loud song and deep praise
We shout out refrain as HE beckons to come ONE and ALL
So let today be the day ETERNITY's secured
IT may be the very last call
Remember this promise: It's never too
    late, HE awaits at the GATE
And beckons us come one and all
To lift up the name of His Son, JESUS our LORD
Who died and came back for us all
Oh, what a day to be living! Oh, what a day to recall!
So as we gather together in love and accord and worship
    our GOD and HIS SON, LET today be the day
    ETERNITY starts life forever be goal number one

VISIONS OF CHRISTMAS

I lie awake on Christmas Eve
Thinking of the joys
That Christmas morn will bring
To all the little girls and boys

Remembering the Christ child
In a manger filled with hay
Near the town of Bethlehem
Of a land so far away

The singing of His praises
The promise of His love
The gifts from kings and wise men
Who were guided from above

The games and toys and packages
Stacked high for all to see
Beneath the lights and tinsel
Of a perfect Christmas tree

The tearing of the wrappings
The shedding of the bows
The shouts of joy and laughter
And the oohs! And ahs! And ohs!

45

The smell of Christmas turkey
And the scent of fresh baked bread
As all gather 'round the table
For the blessing to be said

The flickering of the Yule log
Casts a warm and glowing light
As the day fades toward the shadows
Of a peaceful Christmas night

With memories left to treasure
And forever to endear
I close my eyes to peaceful sleep
For Christmas morn draws near

ALIAS EGO

If you're looking,
To really succeed in life,
Build highways up to the sky,
Get rid of the three best friends you have called,
Me, Myself, and I,
More wonderful plans have been shredded,
Ideas left to deny,
Because of those traitors within us,
Called Me, Myself, and I,
So follow the mission before you,
Is not easy to do,
So you'll see,
To get rid of these friends that adore you,
Called I, Myself, and Me.

ODE TO SILENCE

Eternal silence that surrounds my world,
You challenge my very existence
You drive my will and resolve to learn
You comfort me through the silence of my slumber
You enhance my awareness of surroundings
You build my inner strength to overcome adversity
You position me nearer to my God
For does not a special angel watch o'er the silence?
And though I see the graceful beauty of a bird,
And yet, hear not its song, I ponder not the reason why
For who but I and God both know
      my special gift unfound?
I see and touch and smell the flowers
      and need not hear a sound,
I see and feel the raindrop and the snowflake
      cools my cheek in silence,
The freshness of the air on which they
      float caresses my nostrils,
My life, therefore, I understand can be no less
Or greater than the way I wish to make it,
For I alone must have the will to go that extra mile,
And even though I receive not love, yet give it
And am frowned upon, yet smile, my contribution
To the world will surely be worthwhile.

THE RAPTURE OF
THE CHURCH

You'll see some movement in the clouds
The Christ with saints appear
His second coming in the clouds
The meaning crisp and clear
Is shouted loudly o'er the earth
So none will fail to hear
And those who are alive and well
Will meet Christ in the air
To be with Him forevermore
His loving words to share
We'll reap the harvest
God has sewn for those
Who love and care
Eternity awaits them all
Christ's love is always there

September 17, 2022

THE SAME YESTERDAY, TODAY, AND FOREVER

Eternity stretches before us
His Word is the infinite glue
That holds *His* creation together
And all things of old are made new
He's the same yesterday, today, and forever
And the God in whose image we've grown
So worship, and praise, and adore Him
For heaven will be our new home
His universe ever expanding
As the blessing around us renew
The one thing that never is changing
Is His love that's for me and for you
So trust in His promises coming
And His word as the infinite glue
He's the same yesterday, today, and forever
And He's coming for me and for you.

October 1, 2022

50

LOVE

Love is patient
Love is kind
Sometimes passionate
Sometimes blind
But can you fathom life indeed
Without this gentle want and need
It is the glue to seal and bind
Relationships for all mankind
A special feeling from within
That God extends creation's man
There's nothing like it understand,
it is *His* gift to honor man.

October 1, 2022

TREASURED MOMENTS
TO REMEMBER

Treasured moments passed before us
Never to be lived again
Like the weathered leaves of forest
Carried on the winter wind
So it be that we must savor
All the treasured moments passed
Till our life on earth is over
And the final die is cast
Kneeling at the throne of judgment
Reaping that of which was sown
Praising God and all His glory
Awaiting our new heavenly home
Throngs of angels singing softly
Soothing songs erase all fear
As we look into our future
Our soul's eternal journey nears.

October 1, 2022

MY SOULMATE FOREVER AND REUNION ONCE MORE

I know up in heaven in the files of mankind
Our life record together stands out over time
And out of this life that is one of a kind
His love and protection were oh so divine
While enforcing His word over eons of time
With legions and legions of angels
For His promise is given
And projected from heaven
In His holy word written
Hebrews 9:27
My experience with death
Will happen no more
As I wait the translation to His golden shore
To join with my soulmate
To love evermore.

October 1, 2022

LOVE OVERFLOWS

I received this message of love from my Nina,
The message so deep no one knows.
I'll treasure forever these words from her heart
But were written in love by her toes,
Those words of true love—oh, how precious to me,
Forever engraved on my soul.
As I travel the eons of time up ahead,
Exploring creation untold,
Those words of true love that were so divine
And will weather the eons of time as it flows
Came straight from a heart that was so filled with love
And miraculously written by toes.
Oh, Nina. Oh, Nina. Oh, Nina, my dear,
Your message to my heart overflows.
This treasure to me that will never depart,
For it's deeply engraved on my soul.
Those words of true love that were straight from a heart
But miraculously written by toes
Will weather the storm and erosion of time
And will lift me forever—I know!

THIS POEM AS A MEMO

I'm writing this poem as a memo from God
Of His plan as it's meant to be true
There seems to be a great misconception
That heaven's a world of magic voodoo
But remember His words of beginning
And His plan to then follow through
"*Let's* make man be in *our* image and likeness"
And form creation for something to do
Everything that He planned and created
Was from magnificent wisdom and knowledge
That He, and only He, had unlimited access to
So there's nothing magic about eternity and *heaven*
It was all formed in God's logical mind
His creation of *seraphin* and *angels*
Is to serve *Him* and all of mankind
Though they exist in another dimension
And are invisible to us, that is true
But it eliminates significant confusion
With all that flying around that they do
God has no magic wand that He uses
Everything is formed from His logical mind and
    based on His wisdom and knowledge
To benefit all of mankind

So take this poem as a memo of God's plan to
　　be truth, to be proven o'er eons of time
For there's nothing to surpass *His word* and *His laws*
That can govern the life of mankind
Oh, what a time to be living—oh, what a time so sublime.
　　For there's nothing to surpass *His word* and *His laws*
That will govern the *life* of mankind

WOMEN OF BEAUTY, WOMEN OF GRACE!

The Helpmate God Made for Mankind

From Genesis 2:23

Oh, bone of *my* bone and *flesh* of *my* flesh,
God made you a *helpmate* for man
To share His ways and be part of the life that
    was ultimately the goal and His plan.
I praise Him today for that decision of love,
For what would life be for all of mankind
Without women to hold, to love, and to touch? To
    garner the mind and miraculously find
A helpmate as such, so sublime, and to treasure our
    memories that were shared through the years
    Indelibly recorded on the eons of time,
Yes, I praise Him today for that *love* so to share
    and the helpmate He sent o'er the years. And
    now as we enter the time that is called
The treasure of life's *golden* years,

Take time to give thanks for the wisdom of *God*
   and that decision He made in His plan,
For where would man be without "the bone of
   my bone and the flesh of my flesh"?
Genesis 2:23, *God forbid!*
The answer—of course, there would be great remorse,
   and *man* would have just one more *rib*,
So take a moment of time, give honor and thanks
   to the one called the Great I Am so sublime.
This treasure, He planned when He first created man,
   took Adam's rib, and made a *woman so* fine, so
   fine, His greatest blessing bestowed on mankind!
For where would *man* be without that beautiful
   helpmate, that treasure throughout our lifetime?
So is the question to hold while the obvious unfolds,
   "up a *creek*, without a paddle through time."

POEM

Procrastination, the Word of the Day

We all have this tendency in life's sweet array
To take the easy way out as we face each new day
DELAY TILL TOMORROW, THE TASKS OF TODAY
That word *procrastination* is in our vocabulary to stay
But wait just a moment, who started this thing?
Could GOD be the culprit in His promise to bring
The return of HIS Son to redeem one
    and all and keep us from
Temptations soft fall? There's a reason,
    I'm sure, that the task of today
Is well on its way! HIS word is HIS bond, so to say
Procrastination's a word that's implanted in the SOUL
A part of our vocabulary to stay, but who do
    some blame, but THE CREATOR OF ALL
As we await the return of OUR LORD
GOD's task of today becomes tomorrow's delay.
    Is procrastination the reason unknown?
For we trust in HIS word, as we answer the call

Our Lord's coming to greet one and all! Yes,
    we trust in His word, but not today
So I've heard; will it be winter,
    springtime, summer, or fall?
The answer, of course, is His timing and
    promises found in the scriptures
Procrastination is man's creation and call,
    for God knows of all things
Past, present, and future, no need to delay, for
    His speaking of the word does it all!
Let's be honest and say that it's just man's lazy way
It puts things in disarray of responding to what needs to
    be done; so never, never delay that task till tomorrow
There's no promise tomorrow will come!

June 04, 2023

THE FUTURE TO UNFOLD

Born into poverty, born into sin yet destined
     for greatness and a life with no end
That's the promise eternal from His Holy Word
And given so freely with love
This gift that is offered to all who will be
The children of God from above
So ponder these words of His wisdom to share
It will make or break life in the end
He sends His son, *Jesus*, to beckon you. Come
     for His council; there's no greater friend
So come one and all. This may be the last call;
     only He knows the beginning and the end
This message of love that is sent from above
     is intended for all who would hear
The time of the end He projects that will come
Is rapidly approaching and near
So ponder these words of great wisdom to share
They will make or break life in the end
And rely on the council of *Jesus*, His Son, for
     in Him, there is no greater friend
So let today be the day your future's secured eternity
     awaits in the end, and rely on the wisdom
Of *Jesus* who calls, for in Him, there is no greater friend

GOD'S PROPHESY YET TO COME TRUE

This poem that I'm writing is not fiction
But God's prophesy yet to come true
With many years left yet to cherish
And it seems like there's
Nothing to do and you look at the schedule
Before you then decide to go back to your room
Remember my story and vision from God
When He told me
"I'll send her to you"
That was not only a vision and a dream He sent me
It was a prophesy yet; He'll come too
For God has His ways of working things out
And His word is His bond ever true
So I'm here to the end until He shows the way
And you choose what is offered and true
Companionship, love, and happiness divine
With guaranteed plenty to do
Everyone sees my love for you overflowing
That is, everyone sees it but you
So I'm patiently waiting as God works it out
He's promised this love will come true
You've tried every way to resist and stay friends

Your courage is on full display
But try as you may, God wins in the end
And His word is His bond so to stay
For God keeps His word when it's heard or unheard
And I know you have heard it for true; He told
     me as sure as I'm writing this verse
"Go to Greensboro. I'll send her to you"
So what do I do, for I trust in *the Word*
But have patience—that's all I can do
For I know that for sure, His word is His bond
And His prophesies always come true
Hallelujah! *Hallelujah*! *Hallelujah! Praise* God for
     His prophecies that always come true

GOD RULES THE DAY

You can try as you may to suppress that great smile
And His love-light that shines from within
But try as you may, you'll find God has a way
And our love's here to stay to the end
Now the end's far away to eternity's day
So the smile and the love-light will stay
What a blessing to be when He brings you to me
And that blessing is not far away
Yes, try as you may, you'll find God rules the day
And your smile and His love will ascend
He's never lost yet a battle for love
So it's true He will win in the end
Now God loves your spunk—that's why you were chosen
For this time and this place so to send
His message of truth that is coming our way
For His children, life, and love have no end
Hallelujah! Hallelujah! Hallelujah! Amen
Hallelujah! Hallelujah
Amen

THE WORD OF LOVE
AND HEALING

This poem of love and healing
Is sent to you by me
Each night I pray in sincere faith
To God on bended knee
I ask of Him to heal your mind
Restore those memories
That once great gift now gently fades
God's healing love is free
So every night I go to God
In prayer on bended knee
And ask this prayer of love and healing
That's sent to God and meant for you by me
On bended knee, in faith and love
I ask this prayer to be; set her free, O Jesus, O Jesus, set her
    free
Just touch the soul and heal the mind; bring back the
    memories
In *Jesus's precious name, I pray*
Hallelujah! Hallelujah! Hallelujah! Amen

ANOTHER DAY, ANOTHER TIME, A MEMORY TO ENHANCE THE EARLY '50S

When I was a young soldier, way back in my prime,
It was *wartime*, and preparedness was the call
    of the time. I trained new inductees on
    how to survive in combat, survival
To put their lives on the line, and many
    young men that I trained,
They were Blacks that answered the call from
    their country and would not be coming back
    but would sacrifice willingly their lives.
At the end of the day, we would all shout
    hooray and let our hair down
And grab a bus into town, but sad to say, when we
    boarded the bus, there would be a sign that
    would say "Blacks to the back of the bus."
Now needless to say, after spending all day with
    these patriots who put their lives on the line
Would I be riding up *front*, and I'd happily
    ride with my pride by my side and those
    friends *in the back of the bus.*

It was such a bad *law* that would soon see its flaw
    and be rescinded throughout our great land.
But my memories retain those sad days of *old*,
    and I honor those memories to say
I would still *ride in the back of the bus* with those
    patriots of *color* to the end—with great
    pride hand in hand to defend our *great land*
    and our motto, "In God We Trust."

ABOUT THE AUTHOR

Virgil Sturgeon
Born: October 13, 1931
To: Arnold Curtis Sturgeon and Marian
Rose (Carpenter) Sturgeon
Birthplace: Sac City Iowa
The firstborn of Five siblings, Three Brothers, Two Sisters

Born during the heart of Our Nations "Great Depression" and the natural disaster, within our nations mid-section and farming community of the 1930's that turned our rich farmland into what became known as the "Dust Bowl". Millions of people were without jobs and searching for ways to feed their families, across this great nation. It was, during those trying days, that the Sturgeon family consisting of Arnold, Marian, and two boys, Virgil and Larry, loaded up with all there earthly belongings, packed in a 1929 Chevrolet club coupe and headed West to the state of Oregon, where an overabundant supply of virgin timber was the providing source for a new industry, just beginning to materialize and become a saving grace to our nation's industrial needs. The manufacturing process for the plywood industry. Millions of families were drawn to this new promised source of income, in this time of great need. It was like a magnet, of sorts and in fact, so many hungry people converged on communities like Coquille Oregon, that housing requirements could not be met and "Tent cities was the answer of the times. One of the first Plywood Manufacturing Factories was being built in Coquille, Oregon, and that is where the Sturgeon family settled and lived for 6 months in a large tent with only dirt floors. It became an exciting adventure for the two young boys. From that moment on, Oregon, provided the natural resources and learning opportunities for two young boys, eager to insert themselves in the relatively UN-inhabited, and untamed environment. It provided many learning opportunities for two young boys eager for excitement, directly involved with "mother nature".

It was in communities such as this that Virgil received his "out of school education ", communing with mother nature and GOD's natural surroundings. Oregon was his home until after his high school graduation, and then forgoing college, entering the US army at the outbreak of the Korean War.

Virgil's first poem, was written as a senior in high school, titled "A MOUNTAIN STREAM" He received a grade of A+ for his effort (The poem included in his current book), and has been writing poetry, off and on ever since. He is now 92 and still going strong. A second volume of "GODS WISDOM AND VIRGILS POETRY IN RHYME "will be scheduled for publication in 2024. This along with an autobiography, GOD wants him to share with the world "The Untold Story Can Now Be Told ", coming soon! STAY TUNED!

Printed in the USA
CPSIA information can be obtained
at www.ICGtesting.com
CBHW040536250924
14863CB00065B/1576